quantities of Summersdale books are available to
tions and other organisations. For details contact
ne: +44 (0) 1243771107, fax: +44 (0) 1243 786300 or

CALM

Copyright © Summersdale Publisher

All rights reserved.

No part of this book may be reprod
into a machine language, without th

Summersdale Publishers Ltd
46 West Street
Chichester
West Sussex
PO19 1RP
UK

www.summersdale.com

Printed and bound in China

ISBN: 978-1-84953-031-6

Substantial discounts on bulk
corporations, professional associ
Summersdale Publishers by teleph
email: nicky@summersdale.com.

Calm

thoughts & quotations
for every day

Keep your face to the sunshine and you will never see the shadow.

Helen Keller

Nothing is worth more than this day.

Johann Wolfgang von Goethe

There is a serene and settled majesty to woodland scenery that enters into the soul and delights and elevates it, and fills it with noble inclinations.

Washington Irving

Calmness of mind is one of the beautiful jewels of wisdom.

James Allen

*Inward calm cannot be maintained
unless physical strength is constantly and
intelligently replenished.*

Buddha

If you have a fearful thought, do not
Share it with someone weak:
Whisper it to your saddle-bow, and
Ride on singing.

King Alfred of Wessex

A free mind is one which is untroubled and unfettered by anything.

Meister Eckhart

*Peace is not merely a distant goal that we
seek but a means by which we arrive
at that goal.*

Martin Luther King Jr

Be happy in the moment — that's enough.
Each moment is all we need — not more.

Mother Teresa

Freedom from desire leads to inner peace.

Lao Tzu

What does not destroy me, makes me stronger.

Friedrich Nietzsche

Whenever you are sincerely pleased, you are nourished.

Ralph Waldo Emerson

*You cannot shake hands
with a clenched fist.*

Indira Gandhi

*Beautiful music is the art of the prophets
that can calm the agitations of the soul.*

Martin Luther

For the man sound in body and serene of mind there is no such thing as bad weather; every sky has its beauty, and storms which whip the blood do but make it pulse more vigorously.

George Gissing

We think in eternity,
but we move slowly
through time.

Oscar Wilde

*There is no joy
but calm!*

Alfred Tennyson, 'The Lotos-Eaters'

*Let us not look back in anger, nor forward
in fear, but around in awareness.*

James Thurber

Relaxation comes from letting go of tense thoughts.

Frances Wilshire

Those who are at war with others are not at peace with themselves.

William Hazlitt

Never be in a hurry; do everything quietly and in a calm spirit.

St Francis de Sales

Be calm in arguing; for fierceness makes error a fault, and truth discourtesy.

George Herbert

*Our real blessings often appear to
us in the shapes of pains, losses and
disappointments; but let us have patience,
and we soon shall see them in their
proper figures.*

Joseph Addison

It's better to light a candle than to curse the darkness.

Eleanor Roosevelt

Let us follow our destiny, ebb and flow.
Whatever may happen, we master fortune
by accepting it.

Virgil

I count only the hours
that are serene.

Maurice Maeterlinck

No one outside ourselves can rule us inwardly. When we know this, we become free.

Buddha

Nothing happens to any man which he is not formed by nature to bear.

Marcus Aurelius

Be glad of life because it gives you the chance to love, to work, to play, and to look up at the stars.

Henry Van Dyke

A smile is the beginning
of peace.

Mother Teresa

*A cloudy day is no match for a
sunny disposition.*

William Arthur Ward

*Music alone with sudden charms can bind
The wand'ring sense, and calm the
troubled mind.*

William Congreve, 'Hymn to Harmony'

After a storm comes a calm.

Proverb

Fear cannot be banished, but it can be calm and without panic; it can be mitigated by reason and evaluation.

Vannevar Bush

Few things are brought to a successful issue by impetuous desire, but most by calm and prudent forethought.

Thucydides

To the mind that is still, the whole universe surrenders.

Lao Tzu

Withdraw into your inner self. The rational principle which rules there is content with itself when it acts justly, and so maintains its own tranquillity.

Marcus Aurelius

If you are irritated by every rub, how will your mirror be polished?

Rumi

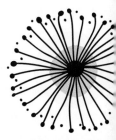

Great necessities call out great virtues.

Abigail Adams

Better than a thousand hollow words, is one word that brings peace.

Buddha

Things without remedy, should be without regard; what is done, is done.

William Shakespeare

Contemplation is the loving sense of this life, this presence and this eternity.

Thomas Merton

Always be kind, for everyone is fighting a hard battle.

Plato

*It was only from an inner calm that man
was able to discover and shape
calm surroundings.*

Stephen Gardiner

Weeping may endure for a night, but the morning brings a shout of joy.

Psalms 30:5

In deep meditation the flow of concentration is continuous, like the flow of oil.

Patanjali

He will easily be content and at peace whose conscience is pure.

Thomas à Kempis

By time and toil, we accomplish more than strength or rage ever could.

Jean de la Fontaine

Nothing in life is to be feared. It is only to be understood.

Marie Curie

In control of desires stillness is attained. In stillness the world is restored.

Lao Tzu

Everything comes gradually at its appointed hour.

Ovid

Quiet minds cannot be perplexed or frightened, but go on in fortune or misfortune at their own private pace, like a clock during a thunderstorm.

Robert Louis Stevenson

Peace is not the absence of war; it is a virtue, a state of mind, a disposition for benevolence, confidence and justice.

Spinoza

The life of man in every part has need of harmony and rhythm.

Plato

If the inner mind has been tamed, the outer enemy cannot harm you.

Atiśa Dipankara Shrijnana

If a man wishes to be sure of the road he treads on, he must close his eyes and walk in the dark.

St John of the Cross

A man of meditation is happy, not for an hour a day, but quite round the circle of all his years.

Isaac Taylor

The pursuit, even of the best things, ought to be calm and tranquil.

Cicero

The Span of Life is too short to be trifled away in unconcerning and unprofitable Matters.

Mary Astell

Cheerfulness keeps up a kind of daylight in the mind, filling it with a steady and perpetual serenity.

Joseph Addison

Do not let trifles disturb your tranquillity of mind... Life is too precious to be sacrificed for the non-essential and transient... Ignore the inconsequential!

Grenville Kleiser

*The ideal of calm exists
in a sitting cat.*

Jules Renard

A peaceful man does more good than a learned one.

Pope John XXIII

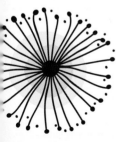

Within you there is a stillness and a sanctuary to which you can retreat at any time and be yourself.

Hermann Hesse

Peace is not the absence of conflict, it is the ability to handle conflict by peaceful means.

Ronald Reagan

To every problem there is already a solution whether you know it or not.

Grenville Kleiser

Work, alternated with needful rest, is the salvation of man or woman.

Antoinette Brown Blackwell

Power is so characteristically calm, that calmness in itself has the aspect of strength.

Robert Bulwer-Lytton

Forget the past and live the present hour.

Sarah Knowles Bolton

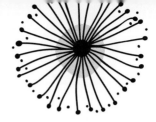

Calmness is the cradle of power.

J. G. Holland

One's action ought to come out of an achieved stillness: not to be mere rushing on.

D. H. Lawrence

Anger dwells only in the bosom of fools.

Albert Einstein

One often calms one's grief by recounting it.

Pierre Corneille

Every now and then go away, have a little relaxation, for when you come back to your work your judgment will be surer.

Leonardo da Vinci

He that can have patience can have what he will.

Benjamin Franklin

Change your thoughts and you change your world.

Norman Vincent Peale

*I exist as I am, that is enough, if no other
in the world be aware I sit content, and if
each and all be aware, I sit content.*

Walt Whitman

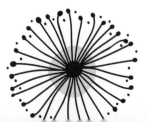

Avoiding danger is no safer… than outright exposure. Life is either a daring adventure or nothing.

Helen Keller

There are always flowers for those who want to see them.

Henri Matisse

You need not wrestle for your good. Your good flows to you most easily when you are relaxed, open and trusting.

Alan Cohen

I am not afraid of tomorrow, for I have seen yesterday and I love today.

William Allen White

Night's deepest gloom is but a calm; that soothes the weary mind:
The laboured days restoring balm; the comfort of mankind.

Leigh Hunt

You will never find time for anything. If you want the time, you must make it.

Charles Buxton

A well-spent day brings happy sleep.

Leonardo da Vinci

He who angers you

conquers you.

Elizabeth Kenny

A heart at peace gives life to the body.

Proverbs 14:30

The more tranquil a man becomes, the greater is his success, his influence, his power for good.

James Allen

Good humour is a tonic for mind and body. It is the best antidote for anxiety and depression... It is the direct route to serenity and contentment.

Grenville Kleiser

*When one door of happiness closes,
another opens.*

Helen Keller

He who lives in harmony with himself lives in harmony with the world.

Marcus Aurelius

Have you enjoyed this book? If so, why not write a review
on your favourite website?

Thanks very much for buying this
Summersdale book.

www.summersdale.com